MW00365819

"I love it! You're an [...] engaging."

"I AM Grateful for the blessing and appearance of Master Teacher Je' Ru, in my life! His profound insight, tutelage, wisdom and guidance has graced me to experience and enjoy the immeasurable benefits of daily transcendental meditation along with ongoing spiritual, mental, emotional, physical and financial growth, elevation, enlightenment and expansion! My purpose and vision of evolving to the best version of myself through self-mastery to support millions of my people throughout the world to LIVE the Best quality of life is literally occurring in the Now-ness of time. I AM most humbly appreciative, honored and encouraged to know that as I move forward on my journey, that I have an extraordinary "Being of Divine Light" illuminating brightly who supports and stands for my highest and greatest good!"

—DeAnna DeWitt,
Founder of Your Sacred Healing and entrepreneur

WEALTH
SECRETS
OF THE SOUL

How to "Be" Wealthy, Healthy,
Opulent & Wise!

MASTER JE'-RU LOVE

Printed in the United States of America

Edited by StudioSteffanie.com Publications
Book interior and ebook design by Amit Dey—amitdey2528@gmail.com
Publishing Consultant: Geoff Affleck—geoffaffleck.com

ISBN: 978-16494556-5-9 (Paperback)

OCC010000 BODY, MIND & SPIRIT / Mindfulness & Meditation
OCC014000 BODY, MIND & SPIRIT / New Thought
OCC019000 BODY, MIND & SPIRIT / Inspiration & Personal Growth

Dedication

—Dedicated to the Beloved—
To everyone who has been taught by me, for your love.
Light, and appreciation
And, best of all, ever-expanding miracle stories.

Table of Contents

Welcome

Thank you, Thank you, and Thank you! Thank for "Be-ing" alive. Thank you for purchasing this book. I hope it will give you inspiration, insight, and an innerstanding of living on planet Earth in a human body, living to the fullest, being awake, aware, and vibrantly alive during these stressful yet wonderful times.

Introduction

A little about me. I'm just your average Black man in America growing up in Chocolate City, Washington, DC, during a time of significant stress. In fact, Washington, DC, has three levels of stress. You have local stress, and at one time DC was the murder capital of the United States. You have National stress with all the federal government: The White House, the Capitol, and the Senate. Then you have the international stress with all the embassies of the World, and the Pentagon.

So, I grew up in an area that's called Adams Morgan, and at the time it was considered "the ghetto." You had to be in gangs to survive. I survived and I'm blessed to share this book with you. I was one of the few people in my family that went to college. In fact, I ended up going to the "Harvard" of black schools, Morehouse College, in Atlanta, Georgia. It's the same college that Martin Luther King attended.

Morehouse has a long history and tradition of producing great leaders in the black community, but it was still a college and part of a conglomeration of historical Black colleges and universities (HBCUs). In fact, Morehouse was part of the AU Center. The AU Center consisted of Morehouse College, Spelman College, Atlanta University, Morris Brown College, and Clark University.

Colleges and universities can be very freeing to someone for their first time out of the house and away from home. So, not only was I learning about higher education, I also was partying and experiencing hallucinogenic drugs and marijuana. In fact, I got so involved with drugs, I became a drug dealer. To rationalize it in my own mind, I only sold the soft drugs: marijuana, MDA, psilocybin, and hashish. I stayed away from cocaine and heroin. Having experiences of Altered States of consciousness opened up my awareness.

Fortunately, I didn't get stuck and become dependent on outside sources. In fact, it made me start looking at natural ways to open up my awareness to become more awake, aware, and vibrantly alive, which led me to meditation. I found that meditation is a natural way to go within yourself to experience higher states of consciousness, dissolve stress in the physiology and the nervous system, and live 200% of life: 100% of the inner and 100% of the outer.

I was just an average student getting by and then I started meditating. I only went to class two times a semester, midterm and finals. I made the Dean's List. Not only that, I ended up going to graduate school at

Howard University in DC, my home. I also ended up going to Ethiopia, Africa. At the base of the Blue Nile I became a teacher of Transcendental Meditation, which changed my life forever. Fast forward to today and I am a full-time certified teacher of Transcendental Meditation, formerly the program director at the Transcendental Meditation Center for the ark in Southeast Washington, DC. I'm also a new age minister with a DD (Doctor of Divinity) degree. I'm also a genuine wealth, life, and spiritual coach for individuals and businesses.

I have two master's degrees and an undergraduate degree in mathematics. So, I went from talking slang and barely able to have a coherent thought in my mind to being highly educated. However, my real life education has come from teaching, training, and coaching people about the true nature of life and helping people to be the best that they can be.

Now, if you picked up this book based upon the title or recommendation from a friend or family member or co-worker, then you're probably experiencing quite a bit of stress in your life. If you're the byproduct of a stressed life, like being tired, or not having clear direction or passion in your life, know that you can accomplish way more and that you're not living up to your full potential. I'm here to tell you that you can accomplish more because I'm coming from a gangbanger's background that was raised by my grandmother and barely saw my parents. They we're going through their own challenges. Between my mother and father and before my 16th birthday, there were six marriages between them – each had three.

All of us know that there is more to life, much more to life, yet very few of us know how to attain it and realize it. I have learned from my experience that we as human beings on Planet Earth, with a nervous system, have greatness within us. We also have the unified field within us, the field of all possibilities within us, or as the great sacred book has said, "The Kingdom of Heaven is within." No matter what your past was, no matter what your present is, and no matter what your future will be, when you step into your kingdom (your consciousness), if you create coherence in your brain and get out of your amygdala (the fight or flight part of your brain), then you can realize your full potential.

The aim of this book is to guide you and help activate you to your highest and greatest Self - the real you. Within these pages there's an activation going on. There's an energetic level that can wake you up to be cosmically conscious right here, right now. We all can live a truly awakened life full of love and radiating light that's overflowing with bliss. I know this is a bold statement. We all sometimes find it's even hard just to get out of the bed in the morning. For some people, just making it down the street is a challenge. Yet there is magnificent beauty to experience on Planet Earth depending on your state of consciousness.

It is truly a "field of all possibilities," but you must realize it. That's what enlightenment means: that you are in the light; you are out of the darkness. The perfect and harmonious functioning of the mind and the body are to bring about a holistic state of consciousness and maintain a natural state of happiness. Like my friend, Marci Shimoff, who wrote the book, "Happy for No Reason," just for being. Re-member that we are human beings, not human doings. We have to go through things and this is true. However, if we elevate our perception into a state of being, a higher state of functioning, then we experience coherence from the front to the back and from the left to right of the brain where the body is superfluid and free of stress. Even though we encounter stress daily, we can become so resilient that stress rolls off of us just like water off a duck's back. We start to experience the world is - As *You* Are!

So, what are we expecting in these pages? We expect insights, inspirations, and experiences from myself and others that I have worked with and have been blessed to help. Also expect some guidelines and techniques because you have something to do. The nature of life with the conditionings of up to about seven years of age only allows a certain type of software to be activated in your computer otherwise known as your subconscious mind.

Throughout the chapters of this book, we're look-ing at reprogramming that computer and putting in the newest, latest, and greatest software so that we can have a highly functioning Peak Performance experience in our lives.

So, we're going to be covering five major portals:

- Portal I is about the Mind.
- Portal II is about the Body.
- Portal III is about Relationships.
- Portal IV is about Spirituality.
- Portal V is about Finances.

Then we're going to put all of that together to show you how this will enable us to live an awakened life, a full life. Live life fully, instead of just living 5% or 10% of mental potential in your day-to-day life. Live 200% of life: 100% of the inner and 100% of the outer.

My mission and vision is to inspire, uplift, and awaken millions of people worldwide to their greatness, magnificence, and enlightenment. I have been assisting and helping people become aware, a way-shower, or guide for over four decades to mainly Black folks throughout the United States and around the world. I have assisted everyone who has come across my path because as you know everyone is pink on the inside. There's only one race - the human race - with various subcultures.

I choose and accept to guide you, to assist you, to tap into your gold mine deep within your consciousness. The deeper you go within, the more fully you live life. The result is that spontaneously your cup starts running over to help your fellow man and woman.

So, the vision of all possibilities is that it is possible to live 'Heaven on Earth,' Back to Eden, Sat Yuga[1], and the Age of Enlightenment. But it's up to us and it starts one person at a time. Hopefully, this book will give you some insight, some understanding, and some inspiration to be the best that you can be and realize your full gigantic, stupendous potential. Let your brilliance and magnificence shine forth now and henceforth forever.

---

[1] Sat Yuga - Golden Age

"One of the most powerful tools we have at our disposal is the human mind. A piece of equipment so powerful that modern science has struggled for years to understand what our Spirit already knows - that our power lies within."

~Master Je' Ru Love

1

Life Is An Inside Job

Life is an inside job. Thank God it is! Because without the inside there would be no outside. Without the absolute, there would be no relative. Without the invisible, there would be no visible. Without the spiritual, there would be no physical. In truth, they are one. But as long as we are in the matrix, the perceived separation is real to the overshadowed observer. But as the true observer, you rise above the lack, the limitation, and the perceptions of limitation. Then you ascend into the greatness of who you really are. And you are an unlimited being with infinite potential.

You are infinitely blessed. You are infinitely rich. You are infinitely well. You are infinitely happy. You are infinitely WHOW (Wealthy, Healthy, Opulent, and Wise)! - We'll talk about that later on in the book.) I am and so are you. By the mere fact of being on Planet Earth, you are the greatest. There is nothing that you cannot be, do, or have.

WAKE UP, WAKE UP, WAKE UP!

So WAKE UP! WAKE UP! WAKE UP to your greatness! And start to live heaven on Earth. Remember "heavens" (the original translation was heavens, not heaven) is a Greek word that stands for expansion. It's the expansion of your mind. So Heaven and Hell are states of mind and your state of mind is determined by your perception. Your perception is perceived in your physical body through millions of nerve ends that go throughout every fiber of your body like antennas. These nerve ends connect up to your brain by way of your neurons, and your neurons firing produce your mind.

So do you want to stay in the lower fight-or-flight aspect of your own self, the reptilian brain, and be in a state of scratching and scrounging and fighting for survival for everything to eke out an existence? To live a life of mediocrity or less? Or do you want to RISE and FLY and get on your Magic Carpet ride and enjoy the Bliss of the absolute, the transcendental joy, and be the best that you can be? We are all born for greatness.

Just like the great Nelson Mandela said, "Our greatest fear is not our inadequacy. Our greatest fear is that we are powerful beyond measure." Know that you are AWAKE, AWARE and VIBRANTLY ALIVE! That YOU ARE Powerful, Invincible, Enlightened and FREE - AHAM BRAHMASMI.[2] Now step into that. BECOME THAT!

INFINITE POTENTIAL WITHIN YOU

Remember: There is infinite potential within you. Just like the flower is within the bud and the acorn is within the oak tree. It's all inside of you – "The Kingdom of heaven is within." More of life wants to come through you. So, instead of trying to do this or that. Instead of working harder. Ideally, you want to find a way to let more of life, more of love, and more of the bliss of who you are, come through you. Allow more of life to come

---

[2] AHAM BRAHMASMI- I AM ever-full or whole.

out of you. It's not out there. That's the Maya Papaya. That's the matrix. That's the fake-out! It doesn't matter outer circumstances, persons, places, conditions or things. There is no power outside of your Self that can determine what you can create and contribute, except for you. You block your own Self. You are the greatest!

YOU ARE THE GREATEST

When Muhammad Ali used to say, "I am the greatest. I'm the greatest." He was declaring that. He was using the power of the spoken word. Yes, he had talent, but he made himself greater and greater by accepting that within his own mind, by going from the level of belief to the level of knowingness. He was way beyond the first level, which is the level of superstition (We'll talk about the 3 levels later on.) and belief, which are very powerful.

You can create based on your beliefs, but beliefs can be erroneous thoughts that are sometimes referred to as the "mistake of the intellect." You are greater than any problem, any situation, any lack, and any condition because you're All-powerful. You are powerful, invincible, enlightened and free. Veda hum. Sat Chit Ananda. Tat Twam Asi.[3] "Know the truth, and the truth will set

---

[3] Veda hum - I Am the Totality
Sat Chit Ananda - Truth, Consciousness, Bliss
Tat Twam Asi - I Am That

you free." Understand that you are the source of all wealth, that you are rich with creative ideas, and that your mind abounds with new original inspired thoughts.

RAISE YOUR VIBRATION

Know who you are and step into that Greatness. You have it all, but you have to realize that and you must raise your vibration. Whatever it is to raise your vibration: meditation, prayer, being in nature, exercise, yoga, eating right, drinking right, taking your body temple to its highest peak performance, and manifesting itself. So whatever you hold in your vision and the process of vision-nering will allow that to happen and to come forth because you are a creator.

You create your own reality. So envision every day. You're creating all the time anyway. You are a manifesting machine. You're creating all the time anyway, but it's up to you to become a conscious deliberate creator. You are the greatest. You're magnificent. You're fantastic. You're marvelous and you are all of it and a bag of chips with a pickle.

2

Open Sesame

Open sesame which is really 'open says me' from my state of self-referral. My ideas and my images impressed out pictured as an expression in 3D reality.

Again, going back to "As above, so below." Also "As within, so without." Whatever you impress on your subconscious mind must express into form or materiality. As we go through these pages, we will be taking a deep dive into opening up to receive everything that you want to be, do, and have.

Now, let me give you a quick introduction in terms of how I woke up from darkness to light, from selfish to selfless, from up to no good to "Be-ing" good, great, and magnificent within my own Self and my cup running over with paying it forward. A series of transformations from substance abuse to deep profound experiences of higher states of consciousness in meditation, to teacher training, to serving others, and literally cleaning my nervous system, to taking the dust off of the mirror so that I could start to have a clear reflection.

I literally opened up the portal in the mountains - Open Sesame - and started to realize and experience that "we create our own reality" and it starts at home. It starts inside. The Kingdom of Heaven is within. The actual translation was a Greek translation and it was "Heavens" with an "s" which means expansion. Expansion of the mind as you expand the mind and open yourself up to your awareness, to your greatness, and to your magnificence.

It blew my mind so much that I dedicated all of my life to giving back the knowledge of the true nature of life. My passion and purpose is to help as many people as I can to realize their full potential and to help usher in and maintain heaven on Earth, one person, at a time.

Just like Pat, who is a retired lawyer and a single parent, who is very successful in life now, but she started off as a down-and-out single mom. I still remember her crying in the back of one of my lectures and I couldn't even see her. I just heard the crying in the background. She had no money, no confidence, and had a young daughter with her. I drove her home and told her to come to the TMC center the next day. She came and she wasn't able to come up with the fee. So, I made arrangements for her to help out around the center. I taught her and her daughter the technique of Transcendental Meditation, TM. She has not, like so many other individuals, realized her full potential.

There are others that are getting by a little better but are still "stressed" out and unfulfilled; some are doing worse, some are doing better. I think there are very few people in the United States of America, (it should be called the United States of Awareness) which is the most prosperous country in the world, who are fulfilled and experiencing fullness. This is all that I am. So when the conditioning in the stress overshadows your being, it's very hard to realize your full potential, your self-worth.

Your self-esteem becomes very small, if any at all, unless you go in and reprogram yourself from all of the negative conditioning and discordant thoughts, words, and behavior. Your life will be a merry-go-round of being unfulfilled. Sometimes you're happy, sometimes you're sad, sometimes you're in the middle, but most times you're unfulfilled.

Now, we're about to explain the five portals to get some insight, information, and knowledge. The first portal being "Secrets of the mind." First of all, Pat, my student learned a meditation technique, Transcendental Meditation, that allows her to go deep within her mind passed the conscious thinking levels. She also learned how to create more coherent thought processes in her brain.

We actually have a physical machine and if it's running properly at Peak Performance then it's manifested in your day-to-day life. You start to find yourself doing less. You start having insights - creativity bursting from your own mind and blossoming within your heart. You start to find that you have higher clarity, clearer vision, and Peak Performance. You find out your mental health has improved and that your mind/body coordination becomes more superfluid. You experience coherence instead of being more of a separate individual with all these various parts. You find that you become a more holistic balanced person. Your mind and the body start to correlate.

Pat found herself going right into the second secret – "Secrets of the Body." This is having that Mind/body coordination working in tandem with the mind, allowing the body to experience perfect health, and allowing the biology of belief to start to stand in that success. You command greatness and believing and knowing and expecting that life is good, great, and magnificent. Knowing that everything that you want to be, do, and have is possible. Knowing that you can do is the first step towards achieving greatness, which we can all do. As Yeshua said, "Ye are Gods and you will create even greater works than I."

As the mind and the body develop, we start going to Portal 3, which is the "Secrets of Relationships." The greatest relationship is with yourself. Pat learned how to better relate to her daughter than to herself and to people in general that she knows. She previously felt abandoned and depressed and now she is more in tune with herself. She went back to school and started dealing with fellow students and her social environment. Before she was just down and out, burned out, didn't want to deal with anybody and was crying. What an incredible turnaround just by curbing unto herself and creating possibilities again and again.

She was tapping into that inner greatness and having the experience of what I call the "Holy" Experience, being an acronym: High On Loving You and that's loving yourself and loving all others. Then as we look at her through the lens of spiritual secrets, we saw that she was tapping into her creative intelligence. She was strengthening her thought forces as she was realizing and manifesting her dreams by strengthening her thought force and dissolving the stress in the physiology, specifically the nervous system. The nervous system is your vehicle for perception.

She started to contact the higher parts of her brain. She started experiencing brain illumination, which we're going to talk about later on in the spiritual secrets. But just to give you a little insight that the brain illumination actually lights up your brain and activates gray matter that normally is not used. So you start to use more of yourself and you start to become more within yourself and that's one of the insights into the term enlightenment; because your brain is lit up.

Your nervous system is not covered in stress and strain and dust and dirt. So it can be luminous. We're really multidimensional-light beings having a human experience. We'll get into that later. I know I just dropped a bombshell, but hopefully, by reading this book and applying some of these techniques, you will have that understanding. You will have that inner-standing that can lead to that experience and knowledge. So you can start achieving the higher parts of the brain, start radiating greater thoughts, and staying out of the negative discordant thoughts. And literally start developing your spiritual body.

We have five bodies that we usually only focus on in the physical but these five portals represent your mental, emotional, physical, spiritual, and financial bodies. Then Portal 5 – "Secrets of our Financial Freedom."

We see Pat going from government assistance (welfare) to becoming a highly paid lawyer. Going from zero to hero and going from not having enough money to eat or catch the bus (back in those days in DC-the Streetcar), to having an abundance of money, wealth, and riches with no concern about lack and limitation. She went from scarcity consciousness to prosperity consciousness. She learned how to apply those things in her own life plus teach those lessons to her daughter.

In my own personal experience of all the five portals, I experience the crystal clear mind of the universe in my daily life, which is phenomenal. I'm so blissful and grateful to 'Be' alive. It is a new glorious adventure. Every day in every way I am living more of a wealthy, healthy, opulent and wise life - a WHOW life. I have been fortunate to experience decades of meditating and doing regular practices (rituals) every day that raise my vibration, therefore raise my consciousness. I see, feel, and experience the world in a whole different light. Regarding my body, I'm in better shape than I was 40 years ago.

I literally feel that I am awake, aware, and vibrantly alive. My "biology of belief" is causing my body to feel younger as opposed to feeling older. In fact, when I'm with my two grown sons, most people think that we are all brothers, which is a great compliment. I have to remind them sometime that I'm the daddy. Then there's the mental, emotional, physical, and financial Secrets of the Mind, Secrets of the Body, and Secrets of Relationship. I have the greatest relationship with myself and with my family and friends and associates and life itself. I'm very happy and fulfilled. Most of the time I walk around happy for no reason because my happiness is not based on external conditions that are always changing.

The nature of life is change. Yet, when you get caught up thinking that things have to be a certain way, that's when you set yourself up for nonfulfillment. I've empowered my Higher self, not my lower self; therefore, "Fullness is all that I am." I'm living a much-fulfilled life from the inside out. From the spiritual Level, I innerstand and have direct experiences to know that I am still growing and expanding within my own 'Self' - that other 90% to 95% of my 'Self.'

It's beautiful tapping into that Creative Intelligence within and allowing my mind, body, and spirit connections to blossom in my everyday life. As a result, wellbeing has been a major benefit in my life. I move throughout my world naturally manifesting abundance, which brings about financial freedom. It has been good, bad, and ugly, but inside I have always remained full of love, light, and bliss. In many experiences, I have literally experienced being in this world but not of it, which is a phenomenal experience. I know my source of supply and I don't get it mixed up with various channels.

So, let's talk about the awakened life. Most people are walking around asleep, even a bunch of them are considered the dead walking. So, it's time to wake up, wake up, and be awake, aware, and vibrantly alive. Let's turn some pages and begin.

As we get into the next chapter, let's see how meditating regularly dissolves stress in the nervous system by opening up Pat's mind and balancing out her mind, body, and spirit connections and clearing up her thoughts. I'm focusing on what she wanted as opposed to what she thought she could get and dealing with PMA, positive mental attitude. She was able to finish school.

She went back to school and only finished undergraduate school. She went on to law school and received a law degree. So she went from barely getting an education with a high school degree to a graduate law degree. She really got her life together and thereby helped her daughter to get her life together. Initially she was depressed, down and out, jacked up and not contributing to society. She required assistance and felt very unworthy. She went from half of an uplifting, happy successful person that raised her daughter on her own, to getting a great job with the government.

She became an immigration lawyer and moved out west to Washington State. She raised her daughter and her daughter became an assistant professor at a HBCU black college. They're happy and they have a much more fulfilled life. Remember the formation of the declaration of fullness is all that I am. And just like when you're having a bad dream with monsters coming after you, when you fall off the cliff, what happens when you wake up? It's a different reality and you realize that you had only been dreaming. That's what we're going to attempt to do in this book. I hope you wake up, enjoy life to the fullest, so you can live a different reality. Live a reality full of goodness, greatness, gratitude, magnificence, and experience all the things that are lovely and true. Now that we've covered all of the portals and an overview, let's jump in and get more detail. So, let's start with Portal 1 - Secrets of the Mind. The mind is much more powerful than the body. In fact, in the seven hermetic laws, the first law is "It's all Mind." In the principle of mentalism, there's but one mind, one power, all the Mind. We use the same mind and power in our individual worlds that the Creator did in creating the universe.

3

Portal I—Secrets
of the Mind

QUANTUM THOUGHT

"Thought rules the world." Emerson and "What you think, you become." Buddha Quote. Very few people think. Most people regurgitate their conditioned thoughts through habituated routines that stretch back to their childhood. When you were a child, you were literally born "wide eyed and bushy tail," meaning that you are open and receptive to everything in your environment from your parents, TV, radio, and teachers. Now that's the internet, video games, internet marketing and society at large that you are in.

The Great Psychiatrist, Carl Jung, refers to it as the "Collective Unconsciousness." Your job as a mature evolving adult is literally to get out of the Matrix, because you're literally growing or dying, evolving or stagnating, expanding or contracting. There's no in-between. As a spiritual being having a human experience, the choice is to enjoy life to the fullest or endure pain and suffering with a few highlights of fleeting happiness. The choice is happiness for no reason, or sadness, depression, fear, lack, and limitation. You can live in quiet desperation or a life that is filled with adventure.

"Life is either a great adventure or it's nothing." - Helen Keller

You can experience joy, brilliance, greatness, magnificence, celebration and enlightenment along with bliss attacks as opposed to heart attacks. Your experience in life can "BE" awake, aware, and vibrantly alive as opposed to getting old, decrepit, and having something take you out. The new Hu-man is taking charge and becoming a master in all that he or she is. The new Hu-man is awake, aware, and vibrantly alive taking full responsibility for everything that happens to him or her. There are no victims just volunteers in this new reality.

"We create our own reality through our Thoughts." It's just that 90%-95% of the time we are unaware because we are guided from our subconscious mind.

"An outrageous life is created by no mind."

When you go beyond the mind, miracles are there. Create Miracles! You are always creating anyway. Why not create the highest and the best? You become what you think about the most. You have 5%-10% mental potential.

Imagine that you are attempting to play the piano with one of ten fingers. You can only hit that piano and make a little tune, but you could never master that piano because you just don't have enough fingers to do it with. Now, life is similar. When you're only using only 5% or 10% of your mental potential, which is analogous to using one of ten fingers, you can only hit life. You can never master it. You can never create a great concert or a symphony or concerto because you just don't have enough. It's the same way with the Mind. You're functioning on a very limited basis. So that's why it is so important for you to take the time to "Know thy Self," to realize your full potential.

In fact, all the great sages, shamans, masters, and gurus have said over and over again for millennials that the greatest and the highest thing that you can do for yourself, for your family, for your city, your nation, and your world is to work on yourself. Work on yourself because we're all affected. We're all connected through what quantum physics calls the Unified Field. And when you affect one part of the field, it affects all the other parts.

So remember, the highest and best thing you can do is constantly *w*ork on yourself. Raise your vibration. Realize your full potential and allow your brain to go into high coherence and start functioning from your frontal lobe being connected. Allo*w* yourself the realization of having coherence throughout the brain: the front, the back, the left and the right hemispheres.

Go into high coherence and then you start functioning just like you had 10 fingers on a piano. Of course, you have to practice and put some work in, but you have the tools to do it. We can all master life and be the best that we can be, do, and have. But we need to apply the GREATEST Wealth Secret of the SOUL, and use more and more of our mental potential.

One of the greatest Wealth Secrets of the Soul is deep meditation. In fact, I call it the #1 Secret of the Soul. As a Meditation Teacher and a WHOW Life Coach, I see it every day where people are stressed out, caught up into anxiety, worry, tension, depression, and basically stressed out.

If you don't take some time to de-stress yourself, open up your mind, and realize your full potential, you will find that instead of growing and evolving and getting happier and fuller and wealthier, kinder, and more compassionate and loving energetically, you start to experience the opposite of all those high vibrational frequencies. The universe operates on a like-by-like basis or as we say for every action there is an equal opposite reaction. Whatever you put out comes back multiplied. If you're putting out lower vibrations, you're going to get more of it. If you're putting out higher vibrations of love, of life, of bliss, you're going to get more of it. It is a law. That's the way the universe works.

Just like gravity is a law, there are invisible laws of the mind that are just as applicable regardless of a person's gender, regardless of a person's race, regardless of what the person believes in, their religion, background, or whatever. It really doesn't matter for the law is irrespective of persons. So anyone can start to apply the laws and reap benefits. You will then start to live a happier, more fulfilled life of love, light, bliss, contribution and you just have more to give.

You start to have the experience of your cup running over. Every thought you have becomes more magnetic. It has more power, it has more creativity, and it has more intelligence and energy. The creative energies within you start to manifest throughout your mind, body, and affairs. There's no limit to this unlimited creative intelligence coming from your superconscious also known as the unified field. As I said earlier, there are three levels of your mind: there's the conscious mind, subconscious mind, and the superconscious mind.

"The mouth of God is the mind of man."

— Neville

Start tapping into the higher aspect of yourself by tapping into your subconscious that goes directly into your Super Consciousness.

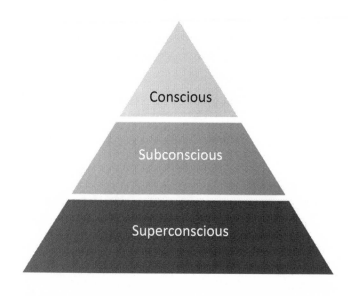

The mind is like a pyramid, where the smallest portion is up at the top. The next biggest portion would be in the middle and then the largest portion is at the base. The top portion would be considered the conscious mind. The middle portion is the subconscious and the lower base is the widest portion which would be your superconscious. So it's up to you to tap in, tune in, and turn on to your Greatness.

Remember, one of the greatest Secrets of the Soul (to make you go WHOW, which is to be wealthy, healthy, opulent, and wise) is to go into deep meditation. I strongly recommend transcendental meditation. In fact, I'm pretty biased because I'm a Transcendental Meditation (TM) teacher. I like to call TM the Rolls Royce of meditation. But just like there are other cars besides the Rolls Royce, you have Chevy's, Volkswagens, and even some Pintos. They still exist. They're all cars but there is a whole other quality to a Rolls Royce.

So, I recommend that you experience the Rolls Royce of meditation. Then you'll naturally start to experience greater things that's in the mind, in your body, and in all of your affairs. If you don't and you let the stress build-up within your system, we find that the energy within the mind starts to go back to an area of the brain called the amygdala, which is sometimes referred to as the reptilian brain. It is associated with fight or flight or freeze. You know how reptiles are always trying to bite something and eat something up. You don't want to be that way. You don't want to stress yourself out. So to go to some of the higher aspects of your own mind, dissolve the stress and in just 10 - 15 minutes of transcendental meditation, you get to a deeper level of rest then you get in 8 hours of sleep.

The mind settles down and the body settles down to about 8% when you go into REM sleep. Your oxygen consumption in metabolic rate would do just 15 to 20 minutes of TM. We find that you go down to a 16% oxygen consumption and metabolic rate. And as you know, if you're running and moving fast, you're going to burn up more oxygen than if you're slowing down.

When you are at the point of REM sleep, rapid eye movement, it takes about 4 hours to get there. We find that in just minutes one can reach that level but they're in a state of restful alertness. Whereas the body's more rested into 8 hours of sleep, yet the mind is alert, aware, expanding and creating coherence. Actually, they've done studies that show people go into what is called a zone, which is associated with high achievement in athletes and successful CEOs when they are solving problems.

What happens is that your brain creates more coherence and your thought force becomes more mag-netized. The effects are immediate and cumulative as your thought force goes into higher levels of coherence every time you sit down to meditate. It is truly a secret and a blessing.

4

Portal II—Secrets
of the Body

Ok, now that we set the stage for the mind, we know from personal experience and scientific validation that the mind and the body correlate. In this chapter, I will show you that when the mind settles down so does the body. The body gets a deep state of rest that has a profound effect on our nervous system, organs, plus our entire physiology as a whole and stress is naturally dissolved. We're going to look at heart attacks vs bliss attacks, brain illumination, the biology of belief, and how we can use it to reverse aging. Also we're going to look at how to be awake, aware, and vibrantly alive.

So, now let's look at Ann who is an artist, painter, and poet who works with elementary programs. One of her main challenges was that she was letting her body die. Her hemoglobin dropped down to 4. Doctors advise that you should be at a 12 for a healthy body. Her body was responding to her mind until I asked her the question: "Do you want to live?" She really didn't want to live so she was dying. But when she thought about it, she said "yes" and then her body started to respond and she started to become alive.

Just the thought, just the attention to be alive, to be awake, to be healthy- now the body can respond in like manner. So one of the main secrets of the body is that the body is its own healing agent. You must command it to do whatever you want or it just picks up from the unconscious collective mind and responds biologically. This is what we call the biology of belief.

Your nervous system has millions of nerve ends that go throughout every fiber of your body like little antennas and connect up to your brain to your neurons. Your neurons are firing and producing your mind, which is not a physical entity. We go to sleep at night and we get up in the morning. Every experience that we have leaves an imprint on our nervous system. You're reading this book, the wind blowing in your face, walking down the street, whatever experience that you have leaves an imprint on your nervous system.

When you get enough impressions on the nervous system the body starts to manifest as being tired. Then nature's natural way of rejuvenating the system is through rest. A good friend of my grandmother called it nature's nurse - that's how the body naturally rejuvenates itself. But in a fast-paced technological society, you can go to bed tired and get up tired because there is always an overload of experience.

That's why it's important to introduce the technology of restful alertness to get the deep rest so the body can rejuvenate itself and dissolve the number one challenge in all of our lives, which is "STRESS." Yet open up the mind so that the mind is alert, aware, and expanding. We have three states of consciousness: waking, dreaming, and sleeping. You're usually conscious in your waking state, which is in a beta realm. Then there is some awareness as you go into theta, which is the dream state, and we're usually unconscious when we go into the sleep state, deep sleep state.

So the uniqueness of this 4th state of consciousness is referred to as restful alertness. The body is more rested than the deepest point of deep sleep, yet the mind is alert, aware, and expanding. In fact, there are scientific studies that prove that during transcendental meditation the body gets a deeper state of rest than twice the level of the deepest point in sleep. However, the mind is alert, aware, and expanding.

The studies were done to compare TM to deep sleep, guided meditation, and mindfulness, which are all good techniques, but they are more on the surface level of the conscious mind. Studies found that the deepest point in deep sleep at REM sleep a person would experience a -8% in oxygen consumption and a -8% in metabolic rate. As you know, if you are running fast you'll increase your metabolism and burn up more oxygen. So when you settle down and get to deep rest, you will use less. It was found that in just 15 to 20 minutes of TM that we were able to go down to -16% oxygen consumption and metabolic rate. That's twice the level of the deepest point of deep sleep and in just 15 to 20 minutes. It takes REM sleep on an average of about 4 hours to get to that point. If you sleep for 8 hours you reach that point twice.

The beauty of TM is every time you sit down to meditate, twice a day every day, in just 15 or 20 minutes, you get to that same level of rest, actually twice the level of deepness, yet your mind is alert, aware, and expanding. This causes the brain to be more coherent. The right and the left hemispheres of the brain go into coherence. The front and back go into coherence and literally start experiencing 200% of life.

This simple but powerful technique allows you to literally pull the bow back, illuminate, and activate more of your brain. You also go way beyond the normal 5% or 10% mental potential that psychologists say most people use at one time. You literally are able to go all the way to the transcendent and pull the bow back 100% and experience what we call pure consciousness. From that level then go into activity. Rest is the basis of activity. The deeper the rest, the more profound the activity.

The latest estimate is that we have over 350 trillion cells in our body. Medical doctors are saying that we have developed a death hormone that we actually believe going back to that biology of belief that a person is supposed to get old, decrepit, age, and die in one's 70s, 80s, and 90s. Very few people live past 100 years. Yet according to modern science the cell never dies. You know the one cell amoeba has been around since the beginning of time for millions of years.

Our physiology is conditioned. There's a "biology of belief" and what we're discussing, teaching, and talking about in this book is how to restructure your belief and then your physiology, your cells, and your organs.

You know every part of your body, your brain, and your stomach. Your skin starts to act in that fashion based on your belief as we know. The mind and the body correlate including the skeleton and things that we think are solid. But as we established in the last chapter and earlier parts of this book, everything is energy, everything is consciousness. So that when you go down to the atoms in a molecule and even to the more subtle particles, you get into the nucleus and subatomic quantum. It's all moving, it's all energy, and it's changing all the time.

We're not as solid as we think, so what causes this aging, this wear and tear on the body that breaks it down into aging and the dis-ease - of course, it's stress. We're in a very fast paced technological society and stress is coming at you all the time 24/7. So we literally have the ability to go in and change the conditioning of the program, and change the death hormone to a life hormone and live indefinitely. That's how powerful we are.

"Our greatest Fear is not our inadequacies. Our greatest fear is that we are powerful beyond measure." - Nelson Mandela

In fact, when anyone asked me how old I am I say I'm ageless and they always say, "You know, come on, tell me old you are." And I say that's my reality- I am ageless." I'm getting younger every day versus aging every day. I'm having bliss attacks every day as opposed to one big heart attack. And as we know heart attacks are an accumulation of stress. Doctors are saying now that 95% - 98% of all diseases are stress related. As a result of the accumulation of stress (distress) certain organs start to break down. The Number 1 killer in the US is heart attacks. By inducing restful alertness (Transcendental Meditation), and getting deep rest, you take away the potential for the heart attack. You reverse the negative effects on the physiology.

Your physiology is its own healing agent. You just have to set up certain conditions and the innate natural ability of your body takes over. We generally look for happiness outside of our self. But as you spend more time within yourself, you get into more of your inner landscape, more stress is cleared, more dust is taken off the mirror, (the mirror being your nervous system) and the dust being the stress. You automatically start to have a clearer reflection and your physiology naturally starts to resort to inner peace, bliss and happiness.

I have a friend who has the New York Times best seller book called, "Happy for No Reason" and that's what starts to happen. You literally start to have bliss attacks. Your system is so calm, peaceful, rested, and relaxed that it is in extreme happiness otherwise known as bliss. I mean literally people had the experience, including myself, of just walking down the street just blissed out, just filled with joy and happiness. So how do you get to this state as opposed to walking down the street and the whole body gives out and you have a heart attack? Then the police comes. You are rushed by ambulance to the hospital. Everyone has to come and support you. You really knocked your whole system over. In fact, your system is literally completely overloaded.

So what we're looking at is setting up a condition whereby taking the rest (nature's nurse) twice-a-day, every day. Allow the body to settle down systematically, once in the morning when you first wake up then get that deep rest. Then about 10 or 12 hours later in the late afternoon and early evening to infuse into your system with that deep level of rest and dissolve the stress. Then you can continue on with your day, evening, and into the night.

People report after meditating, even sleep is better because the whole system is more balanced and calm. Also, many areas improve throughout the physiology that people don't even think about that start to occur spontaneously. It's like watering the root and enjoying every aspect of the tree: the bark, the fruit, the leaves, and the flowers.

There have been a number of studies showing that the brain gets illuminated. Literally gray matter in the brain gets activated and it starts a greater coherence throughout the brain. Your frontal lobe stays aligned and you start to be awake, aware, and vibrantly alive. When your frontal lobe is aligned, you find that the front to back and the left and right side of the brain goes into high coherence. This high coherence is normally associated with athletes when they are in the zone and CEOs when they are solving great problems.

You literally put your brain in the zone twice a day every day. You naturally habituate your brain to stay in that type of success modality. You start to create a success habit within your own 'Self.' Literally your brain is lit up. In fact, the term "enlightenment" in general means that your brain is lit up. The body is stress free and it has allowed for the combination of the mind and the body that brings about a holistic state of consciousness.

A definition of enlightenment is the perfect and harmonious functioning of the mind and the body that bring about a holistic state of consciousness. In general terms you're lit up, you're wired, fired and inspired and you literally are illuminating, and radiating because your body's temple is in such order and refinement. Basically, you're at peak performance and you keep taking yourself there every day in every way.

What we're talking about here is that any person that has a body, a brain, and a nervous system can do this. This is not just for celebrities, top athletes, CEOs and successful people. It's for every person on the planet. We all have greatness within us. We have a marvelous mind. We have a resilient nervous system and a coherent brain if we put ourselves in that format.

Rather than being stressed out, tired, and dull you have a choice. You can be awake, aware, and vibrantly alive all the time by regularly using these wealth secrets and applying the techniques in your day-to-day life. Reinvent your Self. You have the power in your body and mind.

When it comes to aging, an analogy comes to mind. Think about the Model T Ford. They've been around for a long time and once in while you'll see one. The owner of that Model T Ford put that car in the garage and gave it really good care. They kept the oil changed and just really took care of it. Very few people do that with their bodies.

They just wake up in the morning, throw in some food, start to push the body, they get impressions all day, and start manifesting as being tired. They go to sleep at night, pass out, wake up again and push it again. What we're talking about is adding this Wealth Secret of the Soul that naturally allows for deep rest periods during the day while you are still conscious. That's where the whole thing of siestas have come from around the world.

Taking a nap can be helpful, but it's much, much, more powerful to go into a state of restful alertness. Go into the 4th State of Consciousness, which we will be talking about later when we discuss the States of Consciousness. Put yourself in a higher state. You are the 'Master.' You literally have control, but you have to learn how to do this and be disciplined enough to condition yourself to wake up, wake up, wake up!

So, looking at things like the Model T where the owner took very good care of it, you could do the same thing with your physiology. You want to keep your physiology fluid and flexible. The more you stress, you release from your biological framework. The more you keep your system fluid and stretched, the longer it will go.

As a person ages, they allow the process to just keep going. They're allowing the death hormone to take over in their system. Now is the time to create a new reality, re-member, you create your own reality. Take charge now! You are the master in your mind, body, and affairs.

The wear and tear literally tears the body down, but if you keep your body fluid, flexible, lighter and brighter, then it doesn't get tighter and tighter until it just gets solid. You know when a person drops a body they go into rigor mortis.

What we're looking at is one of the Wealth Secrets of the Soul. Keep the body fluid and flexible rather than aging and decaying. Your mind/body creates a "biology of belief." As you change your beliefs, then you change the outer actions, then you can reverse and change the death hormone.

By refining your nervous system, you're getting the stress out of the physiology, and you naturally go into higher performance. There's less emphasis on wear and tear and "fear" - False Evidence Appearing Real. And all of this is being accomplished by the greatest Wealth Secret of the Soul, which is meditation, by being still - "BE STILL AND KNOW I AM GOD."

Science also verifies this through the 3rd law of thermodynamics that states, "When the system goes to absolute zero, the entropy leaves the system, the disorder, the disease, and the disharmony." Entropy leaves the system, the disorder, the dis-ease, the disharmony, and you find yourself vibrantly alive firing on all cylinders.

When the body is balancing itself, you start feeling awake, aware, and vibrantly alive. That carries you throughout the day and then you meditate again in the late afternoon/early evening. That will carry you through to your evening and it carries you through the night. You sleep better, you feel better, and the mind won't be so active.

You feel alive in your body temple. You go from existing to living and use your whole self. Be alive! Don't be the walking dead. As a friend of mine said, "I want to get out of life alive." I know from personal experience that this well secret of the body is real. I have a son that will be 45 years of age this year. In fact, I feel better now than I did when I was in my teenage years and as a young man than I did before. Now I can run up-and-down a basketball court with the best of them. I do yoga every day and when I'm with my sons everyone thinks that we're all brothers. I have to remind them sometimes that I'm the daddy. I'm full of life vim and vigor and I've incorporated celebration in my lifestyle.

We call it meditation and a party, which we literally meditate before the party. There's no alcohol, marijuana, or drugs. We have a group meditation and then we party all night because we have so much energy and we feel so good. So compare that to barely getting up in the morning after partying all night and waking up feeling whole complete, joyous, happy, grateful, and thankful for being awake, aware, and vibrantly alive. This wisdom is helping me more and more every day in every way. I'm able to impact others' lives by sharing this insight and wisdom. So now that we have an understanding of our mind and our body, let's look at our relationships and, of course, our greatest relationship is with our own "Self"", our own "Self"-referral.

5

Portal III—Secrets of Relationships

Now that we've looked at our marvelous mind and our incredible body and how the mind/body coordination brings about our "Self," then the greatest growth and challenge is with our "Self." In fact, the greatest relationship you will ever have is with yourself. There is a great saying, "Curbing on to myself, I create again and again." This is from the ancient Vedic text, the Upanishads.

So, who are you? Why are we here? What is the purpose of your life? You know these classic questions that come up for all of us from time to time. Am I just a bag of bones that is afraid one minute and happy the next, going from fear to love, from young to old, from birth to death; or am I more than that? Am I my mind, body, intellect, ego, or am I the Atman, the soul, the spirit behind all of it? In fact, one of the greatest Secrets of the Soul for relationships is that "I am alpha and omega. I am the beginning, I am the first and the last. Before me, there's no other." I am beyond all those things which we consider ourselves to be.

I'm not the mind, body, intellect, ego, or emotions. I am the soul, the spirit, the Atman behind all of it. I can either get caught up in my ego, which is never fulfilled and always want more and more, or I can be a witness, an observer to the beautiful play and display of life. In fact, a great acronym for ego is "Edging God Out." Edging out your God force, your higher Self, and buying into your lower self-EGO - Edging God Out.

So, we want to exalt and illuminate the God force within us. There are various definitions of God from religions and from the metaphysical and the esoteric. If we were to give a general definition to God as being omnipresent, omnipotent, and omniscience, then where is God not? A course in Miracles says, "Are we going to buy in to the illusion, the Maya, the matrix, or are we going to ascend, elevate, and escalate into our higher Self, into enlightenment, into being a fully realized human being?" And my greatest teacher, Maharishi Mahesh Yogi said, "The world is as you are."

Depending upon your state of consciousness will determine your experience in the world. Do you feel worthy? Do you feel great, magnificent, and marvelous? Or do you experience fear, anxiety, pain, suffering, lack, and limitation? It's all up to you. If you base your feelings on the relationship outside of yourself, because the nature of the relative is always change, you will find yourself always holding the bag, so to speak.

Whenever you try to hold on to something that is forever changing, you'll find that your life will be very topsy turvy, like a leaf blowing in the wind. But you can establish yourself within yourself again through deep meditation and through various ways to raise your vibration, which will be discussed throughout this book.

THE ULTIMATE RELATIONSHIP

You start to be anchored in the truth, in that light, in the truth of God, and the truth will set you free. You can replace God with Universe, Source, or with whatever works for you - creative intelligence, unified feel. It's all the same. That creative intelligent force that creates worlds that creates everything within you and around you and that you Co-create with every Nano second, whether you're aware of it or not, that is the ultimate relationship.

On a physiological level, when the energy at the base of your spine, which is referred to as the 'Kundalini," goes up your spine into the higher nerve ends in the brain, it is the ultimate marriage. The greatest relationship is merging the lower aspect of yourself with the higher aspect of your Self, which is sometimes referred to in ancient Eastern scriptures as: the Divine Connection, the Shiva and the Shakti, the Yen and the Yang. When you can establish that within yourself, when you can take the stress off of your physiology, when you can take enough dust off of the mirror, then you start to have a clear reflection of yourself. In fact, I refer to this as an awakening; to be awake within yourself to be "Awake, Aware, and Vibrantly Alive," otherwise you're literally walking around asleep.

I know you've heard about those movies such as the waking dead. The whole process of re-membering is going from that feeling of lack and limitation where you're feeling separated. As a result there is fear, there is anxiety, and there is a lack of understanding. You don't have any certainty or security. And if you try to get that from the outside it always changes. But you can find it within yourself because remember the Kingdom of heaven is within. Life is an inside job!

NOURISH NOBLE THOUGHTS

So instead of feeding your ego with negativity, lack, and limitation, start to nourish yourself. You'll start to have noble thoughts, God thoughts, marvelous thoughts, brilliant thoughts, uplifting thoughts, and nourishing thoughts as opposed to negative thoughts, as opposed to lack limitation. Instead of feeding your ego, you start to realize your higher Self and become established in that. "I am that that I am." TAT TWAM AST.

Talking about this reminds me of a story about a Native American youth. He was having all of these bad thoughts and he had a side of him that was egotistical and negative and selfish. He didn't like it but it would come up in him from time to time. He also had another side to him which was young and brave with honor, service, and bravery.

So he went to his wise grandfather and said, "Grandfather, I have these two wolves in me: one is a wolf that is greedy and wants to eat up everything. It's selfish and wants to take things from other people and very negative. And then I have this other wolf in me that is kind, generous, brave, uplifting, loving, and that is this really good, nourishing, and loving wolf." He told his grandfather, "I have both of these wolves within me. How do I choose which one of these wolves I should serve?"

His grandfather looked at him very lovingly into his eyes and said, "Whichever wolf you feed the most will be with you, the other will go away." So, the same thing in relationships. If we're loving, kind, generous, and serving selflessly unconditionally, the ego will not grow and your higher Self will flourish. It's up to you; you get to choose. This is a free-will universe. You might as well choose the highest and the best. But it does take some discipline and it takes some application. Apply techniques for personal growth and develop successful habits, which are sometimes referred to as creating rituals that you do every day in every way. And one of the main secrets is to forgive yourself and to love yourself.

FEEL GOOD, LOVE YOURSELF, AND GIVE

I like to use the example of the great soul singer, rhythm and blues singer named James Brown. He has a song called, "I Feel Good." You want to feel good. In fact, there is a great transformational teacher that states that the highest and the best thing you can do in life is to feel good. Because when you feel good you're feeling those higher vibrations, the vibrations of love, joy, kindness, bliss, harmony, and service. These feelings are on a much higher vibration than guilt, shame, worry, and anxiety. You get to choose your state of vibrations.

As a result of choosing your state, you choose your relationship because then right behind that is the emotion and a feeling that is different than an emotion. Emotions are just energy in motion. A feeling is a state; you can choose your feelings you can think from your heart and feel from your mind, it's up to you. You can put yourself in a state of happiness or you put yourself in a state of worry and anxiety. If you don't, someone else, some person, place, or thing will put you in the existing circumstance of the collective unconsciousness. So put your energy in motion at the highest and the best. There's only one description of God in the sacred book, The Bible, and it says "God is love."

So love yourself as James Brown says, "Get back, I gotta kiss myself" and kiss yourself. How do you love yourself and let that love overflow? Let your cup runneth over. When you have an overflowing cup, you naturally want to do Seva, which is contribution. Give back because you have so much to give. Service is the definition of Seva, a Sanskrit word which means selfless service. Serve expecting nothing in return just give, give, give, and give.

One of the greatest secrets of the universe: whatever you want in life, give it. The more you give, the more you receive; and that's the way the universe works - whatever you put out comes back multiplied. Okay, we can say it scientifically - for every action, there's an equal and opposite reaction. We can say it religiously - you reap what you sow. What goes around, comes around. It's all the same thing. The universe works by law. So use this secret and understand that everything is self-referral. So the more you love yourself, the more love is reflected in love for others.

FORGIVENESS

One of the biggest things under relationships is forgiveness - forgive yourself fully and freely. Forgive everyone and everything that could possibly need forgiveness. I am free and they are free too. All things in the past, present, and future, I am free and they are free, too, now and forever. Give for that's what forgiveness means - is to give. We're just talking about give, give, give. When you try to hold on, that's the ego. So let go. Let God release and let go! Clear, delete, and let it go. Let go and let God. Rise up to your greatness, your magnificence, your brilliance, and share it with the world. First share it with yourself and become more loving every day in every way. Then it will reflect in your relationships with others; your family, friends, and associates; anybody you meet in life.

One of the easiest ways to give is with a smile. There have been studies that show that when a person smiles that just the movement of the way the face moves for you to open your mouth and for your teeth to show, it creates a reaction in the brain that starts to ignite happiness and bliss in yourself just by smiling. There are a lot of simple things that you can do, but the main thing to know is that you are your brothers' and sisters' keeper, and it first starts with self-love.

Love yourself and bless yourself. You can bless others. You can add increase to others and also add it to yourself. Remember that the greatest relationship is with yourself. And as you curb back unto yourself, by nourishing and uplifting yourself, you create the greatest love. We're not talking about the selfish, egotistical aspects of love, but taking it to higher and higher levels of truth and understanding of bliss and love and joy and kindness and compassion. In fact, most of the planet is stuck in the three lower chakras.

Chakras are the energetic system that is the basis of your physiology and things such as your emotions and feelings depending on how they are functioning. Chakra means spin. Depending on how your chakras are spinning, they will determine your experience in life. We are energetic beings. Some wise beings say that we are multiple dimensional-light beings and that we have enough energy in us to run an entire city.

There are seven basic chakras in our systems. The first chakra is referred to as the root chakra, which is at the base of your spine. The second one is referred to the sexual chakra, which is for procreation and is around the genitals, and then the third chakra is it you solar plexus, and that deals with your Self or your individual ego as you project yourself in society. Then you move on up to the forth chakra, which is your spiritual heart chakra and you know your regular heart is to the left of your physical heart and this heart chakra is exemplified by compassion.

Then you go up to your throat, which is the fifth chakra. The sixth chakra is between your eyebrows, sometimes referred to as your third Eye. Last but not least is your seventh or crown chakra. So to become a fully realized human being, you have to have all of your chakras open and functioning together and spinning properly. One chakra is no better than the other. Yet, the holistic combination of all 7 of them firing and spinning together brings about a functioning in your mind body and affairs. That is the ultimate relationship.

So, you have all of your chakras in the proper harmonious manner just like the Earth, as we talked about earlier, hurling through space at thousands of miles an hour. The same thing is existing within our own system. Going back to the Hermetic principle, "As above, so below. As within, so without." When you balance the inner system known as the chakras, then you have the perfect relationship within yourself and it is reflected in your day-to-day life with persons, places, and affairs.

Just like my good friend and student, Dr. Rita, learned that you find yourself calmer and collected when you find yourself still and balanced and doing less in accomplishing more. You're not being pulled off of your center and you're able to help others more and thereby helping yourself. You start to find more consciousness and more self-awareness and you naturally start to release negative self-talk, and you find it that your thoughts, words, deeds, and action naturally comes into balance." She found that through a natural process of self-love. She was able to embrace who she actually was.

Remember there's 200% of life: 100% of the inner and 100% of the outer. The average person only uses about 5% of his outer exclusively. So start using the other 90% - 95%. You deserve it. You're completely worthy just by being a human being on planet Earth; you are totally worthy.

Start now to feel better. Be happier, more joyful, more loving, and kinder. It is a choice. You are the master. Start with yourself and choose the highest and the best. A great prosperity teacher once said, "Choose until your good is better and your better's best." In terms of my own life, I was a very selfish self-interest person who was always looking to get love from someone else. As a result I ended up with many girlfriends and being married twice. However, once I started meditating and loving myself from within, from the inside out and being at peace and loving myself and hugging and kissing myself, I'm at peace by myself. And being with someone else is just some icing on the cake. I don't need anyone. I prefer to be with someone but there's a huge difference between needing and preferring. As they say in relationships, "you complete me, you're my better half." But how can somebody else be your better half?

That statement says that you're not whole and no one else can complete you. You're a whole being within yourself. You come on this planet by yourself and naturally you leave this planet by yourself. You need to become fully realized otherwise you're playing the piano with one of ten fingers. You can only play a little tune and hit at the piano as opposed to creating a great concert or Symphony. That's what we're talking about here. Create the symphony of your life. Step into your greatness! Reveal all the secrets and use them. Practice them and live life fully in your own right. Self-hug yourself every day, love yourself every day, and let that love overflow and roll into loving and healing and prospering with everyone else.

Now that we're at 200%, balanced in mind, body, and relationships, let's look at our spirit, our soul, the Atman, the basis of everything in existence worldly and Divine.

6

Portal IV—Spiritual Secrets

Okay, now that we've covered mental, emotional, and physical secrets, let's get into spiritual secrets, which is the basis of who we are. You've probably heard the axiom, the great saying that "we're not human beings having a spiritual experience..." once and a while. "We are spiritual beings having a human experience." Now, one of the most spiritual things you can have is a thought. You can't see a thought. You can't grab a thought because a thought is not physical. A definition of spirituality is that which is unseen, but you can see a thought manifest.

In fact, everything in our day-to-day existence comes from somebody's thought, from somebody's idea. We're constantly creating and having ideas. Now, whether you actualize that idea, that thought is a different story. The beauty of the secrets revealed in this book will assist you to be, do, and have whatever it is that you want. First, we want to start from the cause. Another wealth secret of the soul is that the cause is within your own mind. "Cause," as in *cause and effect*, comes from thought and your thoughts come from your consciousness.

Everything that happens in our outer life, in the relative world, that is "effect." As the ancient text, Emerald Tablets, said, "As above, so below. As within, so without." As we talked about before, we're on planet Earth hurling through space over 1,000 miles per rotation around the sun in this Solar System. This Solar System is in the Milky Way Galaxy. Then there are clusters of galaxies within this universe. It goes on and on, world without end. In fact, scientists are now calling it the Omniverse - Where there are universes within universes and it just keeps expanding. So, another Wealth Secret of the Soul is that in the same way that we go within ourselves and it keeps expanding, it's the same way without.

In fact, there is a classic video, called "Powers of 10" where you see a man on a golf course. He's on a putting green, then you see him 10x out. Then you see him on the golf course. Then it goes out 10 more times and you see the city. It keeps expanding out by powers of 10 exponentially.

Then it shows the state, then it show the United States. Then it shows North America, then it shows the whole world. Then it shows the Solar System, then the Milky Way Galaxy. Then it shows clusters of galaxies, then the whole universe, and then universes within universes. Worlds without end always expanding. Then it comes back to the gentleman on the golf course and then it goes the opposite way showing him as a full person then it goes to his arm, then it goes to a molecule on his hand, then the atoms, and then the nucleus and then the subatomic particles, and on and on. And in that same expression it continues to just keep expanding. So the same expression out there's also inside of you and so and as it goes within you there's an expression of your own consciousness.

Your consciousness is the sum total of who you are, of your mind/body connection; everything you have, that conscious mind which we talked about then the subconsciousness and then the superconscious. Actually, we have evolved from our consciousness being stuck in the lower part of the brain - the Amygdala (fight or flight reptilian brain) to the prefrontal cortex, the CEO of our system that makes decisions, achieves goals, etc., and gives direct info into your subconsciousness.

It is also very interesting to note that your subconscious was actually referred to in ancient times as your heart - the feeling level. In fact, the ancient concept was that as you fully develop your consciousness and take the stress out of your system, you get to a point where you are "thinking from your heart and feeling from your mind." As you develop this inner landscape, it takes you to higher and higher levels of Consciousness. But, until we have expanded our conscious mind beyond the 5% - 10% that psychologists say that we use, we're very limited.

Your conscious mind picks, chooses, and decides. Your conscious mind puts everything in motion like a tape recorder. Your conscious mind turns on the tape, but whatever is imprinted on the tape recorder (subconscious mind) runs the tape. It's just like we said earlier in this book. Psychologists say whatever is programmed in you by seven years old stays with you your entire life and runs the bus no matter how old you are, unless you change that programming through one of the greatest wealth Secrets of the Soul, which is meditation.

That seven years of all subconscious thoughts will run the bus no matter where. Now let's break down your consciousness. You have the waking state, which is in the beta range of about 5% - 10% of your mental potential. Then you have the dream state, which is characterized in the frequency of brain wave functioning called the theta state. That's from nine months within your mother's womb to about seven years.

You're in the theta state all the time. It's like a little duckling following the mother duck. During these years you're in complete imprinting. Next there's deep sleep, which is in the delta range. These are the three main states of consciousness that we function through every day. We're going to touch on the other states of consciousness just to give you an overall understanding, but there will be further books and information regarding this as there are really seven main states of consciousness that are known and experienced by (wo)man and we just touched on the first three.

The 4th state is a transcendental consciousness, (TC), which falls right below beta in a high alpha range, which is a combo of waking and the dreaming states that we refer to as "restful alertness." Where the body is more rested than doing eight hours of sleep, twice the level, yet the mind is alert, aware, and expanding. By having that experience consciously, you have to bring it out into your day-to-day activity.

Now once the restful alertness is established in your waking state, your dream state and your sleep state, we call the next stage of consciousness - cosmic consciousness, (CC), which is referred to by different names. Some people refer to it as "enlightenment." This is where the whole brain is functioning and is lit up as opposed to partially functioning. It's referred to as a fully realized human being.

Some of you might remember Abraham Maslow's hierarchy of self-actualization. We're talking about a fully self-actualized human being. Basically, the perfect and harmonious functions of the mind/body that bring about a holistic state of consciousness, where the observer effect in Quantum Physics is fully in effect. The big Self is separate from all activities. Almost like you're a witness or an observer during the other states. During the waking state, the dream state, and the sleep state, and in this state you really know that you are more than your mind, body, ego, and relationships because you're actually having the experience. There are two more states of consciousness that we referenced here, but I will talk about them more in future books. They are glorified cosmic consciousness (GCC) and Unity consciousness (UC).

Now let's talk about the greatest Wealth Secret of the Soul again, which is meditation. And I'm pretty biased because I teach transcendental meditation (TM). I think that TM is the Rolls Royce of meditation. There are many types of meditation. Meditation just means deep thinking. There are all kinds of meditation. Guided meditation, mindfulness, concentration, and contemplation meditations. You can have meditation with music, meditation looking at the wall, a candle, looking between the eyebrows, or focusing on anything. There are so many meditations. Meditation just means deep thinking. You go into a meditative state, the beauty of transcendental meditation, which I refer to as the Rolls Royce of meditation.

There are a few Chevys, a few Pintos out there, but the Rolls Royce gets you to that deep level of meditation in just 15-20 minutes. This allows for you to function in great activity. You don't have to sit up in a cave for 10-12 hours a day or temple and you can get similar benefits by meditating and acting. Meditating and acting 20 minutes twice a day, every day, flexing the nervous system dissolving stress and allowing the mind to expand and then perform your daily activity at peak performance.

It's literally like a cloth and a dye analogy. Take a white cloth and put in some gold dye, then put it out in the sun and it starts to fade. But every time you put it back in the sun more color will stay in. Then put it back into sun and back into the dye over and over again alternately thereby more color will stay in until its color lasts.

No matter how much sun hits it, it will never fade. So the same thing with meditation and activity. You meditate, then you act, meditate then you act, and meditate and act. As a result, more of that pure consciousness, that restful alertness stays within your system. So, then its maintained 24/7 during you're waking, your dreaming, and your sleeping state. That would be a state of cosmic consciousness or referred to as enlightenment. It's where you literally are lit up. You are wired, fired, inspired. You know you are tapped in, tuned in, turned on and as a result you literally are functioning with high coherence in your brain and super fluidity in your physiology.

You're functioning as a fully realized human being and using all of your God-given abilities within. It's just a matter of going within yourself, tapping your pure consciousness and dissolving the distress in the mind and the body, which will bring about a holistic state of consciousness. But it's up to you. It's your choice to step into your greatness, your magnificence, your brilliance and do the work to get there. It's just like a farmer with some land. He has to go out plant the seed, water the land, make sure there's good sunshine and take the weeds out. The weeds are negative thoughts. The weeds are discordant thoughts within our system. When the weeds effect the ground, and the soil, which is the mind and the body and thus distress. So we have to get the stress out.

Nature's natural way as we stated earlier is nature's nurse, which is through deep rest. We know you can sleep your life away and still be tired, but the deep rest along with the expansion of your consciousness, that's restful, that's alertness, and it's one of the greatest Secrets of the Soul. The Wealth Secrets of the Soul is transcendental meditation, which is a form of meditation what we call automatic self-transcending. It just goes on by itself. All you do is set up the conditions.

Then you have another category that meditation falls into what is called "focused attention," which is referred to as concentration. It's like you holding the mind focusing on the mind and the mind's natural tendency is to flow to fields of greater happiness. Remember, "You are the master of your ship." You can develop your consciousness and thereby change your world! "The world is as you are."

As opposed to just letting things happen to you and then you react, you create the situations in your life. If there is a situation that you do not desire, that you want to change, change it from your level of consciousness. We are literally "Masters," but we must step into our *masterhood*. So the Wealth Secret of the Soul is to own that you are the creator of your reality.

Now let's step into it by using techniques and technologies that can raise our consciousness, dissolve inhibiting factors to decrease dis-ease and the negative thoughts and emotions. Increase your experiences of higher states of consciousness. Instead of having a headache, start experiencing brain illuminations. Start experiencing higher states of consciousness. Start experiencing happiness for no reason. Start to feel within yourself, like a cloud has been lifted from your consciousness.

In my own experiences and thousands of individuals that I have taught, I find myself awake, aware, and vibrantly alive more and more every day. As a result, my level of gratitude and appreciation and thankfulness has increased many fold. I feel that I am a part of this great and grand marvelous experience called life. I feel very privileged to be part of this experience, to be a teacher, a wayshower/a pointer, directed towards helping others to wake up, to be conscious, living embodiments of the greatness, brilliance, and magnificence. That is within you to really be a fully realized human being.

I literally went from being drugged and wearing dark shades at night time to being vibrate, jubilant, happy, and joyous to be around and appreciating nature in everyone around me literally feeling awake, aware, and vibrantly alive. I love myself. I love you.

7

Portal V—Secrets
of Financial Freedom

Now that we have covered mental, physical, emotional, and spirituality, now we're going to cover the financial. As you know in the Western world we don't go out and build our own houses and grow our own food or make our own clothes. We work at a job, a career, or business to create some money and then use that as a medium of exchange.

So let's look at money. M-O-N-E-Y = my own natural energy yield. The beauty of money wealth and riches is that we already have it inside of ourselves. Riches are made with the mind. Everything comes from an idea. One idea can make you a fortune and impact the lives of millions of people. We are only one thought away from financial freedom. The universe is like a genie — "Your wish is my command." We just have to open our minds to receive. King Solomon arrayed in all of his splendor, opulence, and grandeur could not overshadow the beauty of the lilies in the field.

Abundance is the natural state of affairs of the universe. Everywhere we look there is abundance. There is an abundance of stars, planets, universes, of grains of sand, blades of grass, of leaves, etc. There is an abundance of air that we breathe, there's an abundance of water, an abundance of fruit, an abundance of everything. It is the natural state of affairs of the universe. What we will be learning in the financial Secrets of the Soul is that we all have a natural ability to tap into the abundance of the universe that exists within us, all around us, and through us. Tapping into that abundance is one of the greatest Wealth Secrets of the Soul.

Abundance is created in our mind. The Wealth Secret of the Soul is that abundance is created in the mind first. Everything is created twice: first in the mind and then if we can hold the vision, it'll manifest in our day-to-day affairs. The natural state of the universe is abundance and we're going to look at that abundance by applying certain universal laws within our own mind and, of course, some action - some inspired action.

These laws of the mind are just like physical laws (i.e. gravity), but you must know how to use them and not cancel them out with negative thoughts or limiting beliefs. The first law is the law of radiation and attraction is considered the law of laws. Under that law, you start to understand that you can't get something for nothing, but you can always give something. So whatever you radiate in your words, thoughts, deeds, and actions you will attract. As we mentioned earlier, mental preparation comes first and you must be deliberate and definite about your wealth.

Understand that you are magnetic and that every thought is magnetic. The way the universe works is that whatever you put out comes back multiplied. You reap what you sow. What goes around comes around. For every action there is an equal and opposite reaction. So, you want to be deliberate and definite about your wealth because you will magnetize it. You will attract it to yourself as long as you don't have negative thoughts or limiting beliefs. Once you realize that whatever your desires are within yourself, it starts inside. Life is an inside job and then as long as you don't limit yourself with discordant thoughts, negative thoughts, disharmonious thoughts, actions and behavior, then the outer will manifest easily for you as long as you hold on to the vision - to go from a florescent light to a laser beam.

From the unified field that we exist in or whether you want to call it the matrix, it's all the same thing. So what we're looking at doing is taking that wave and turning it into a particle. Taking it from the un-manifested and turning it into the manifest, from the relative to the absolute. You're taking your desires, which are in the form of a hazy, fuzzy, wave within your own mind and then creating them into a 3-D reality, basically like a replicator in Star Trek.

In fact, we have replicators now. One of them is a 3-D printer and they say that scientifically there are already replicators that can create and replicate anything that has already been created. They're just not available for mass use and the cost is too high, but basically you're looking at modern alchemy. You're just moving the atoms and molecules around to create the desired effect.

The classic alchemy is to turn lead into gold. Everything is made up of atoms and molecules, they're just moving at different rates in different vibrations and at different combinations, but they're all made up of the same thing, the same substance, the same consciousness, and the same light. So that's the first law, the law of radiation and attraction. Next, we have the law vacuum. The law of vacuum states that the universe abhors a vacuum, that you want to let go of the lesser to make room for the greater to form a vacuum within your mind. Now, one of the greatest ways to apply the law of vacuum is to forgive. Forgiveness is to release something so there's room for something else to come back.

Release is very magnetic because you don't get something for nothing. You can always give something and you can always find something to give and it starts in your mind. It goes into one of the other laws of increase because with the vacuum law, you want to look up towards prosperity and not down towards lack and the limitation and guilt and shame and worry. Also, you want to always put you best foot forward. Knowing that that radiation in that vibration will allow for you to create a vacuum.

One story along that line was a lady who was very wealthy that had a husband who died and she didn't have to manage their finances. She left everything up to her husband and when he passed, she didn't have any more money. So she had to be creative and she had one good dress because she had pond all of the other dresses. She had taken them into assignment shops. She had pond everything including the furniture. She was down to one really good dress. She literally didn't have any money, but instead of panicking she just washed that dress every day and wore it like it was a really fine new expensive dress.

She didn't tell any of her friends that she didn't have any money. She literally called up her friends and convinced them to invite her out to lunch or dinner with them every day because she had literally lost all of her money. She didn't have money for food, overhead, anything, but she maintained that high vibration and went out with her friends and ate very well at some of the finest restaurants. Then one day she was sitting at a table and dropped something.

A gentleman sitting at the nearby table bent over and picked it up. Their eyes met and before you knew it, they were dating and in a short period of time he asked her to marry her, and he was a wealthy gentleman. So she was back into her prosperity and abundance. The beautiful thing was she never lost her prosperity consciousness and she never bought into scarcity consciousness. So as a result even though she had created a vacuum, she never lost her prosperity consciousness and didn't buy into appearances through scarcity consciousness. Always put your best foot forward knowing that the universe is the source of your supply and always has your back.

The next law is the creative law. And under the creative law we want to look at a strong desire to bring us success and power. We want to write down our desires and understand that prosperity is a plan, a result. The third law is the creative law of prosperity, which is a strong desire. Write down your desires. Prosperity is your birthright. Make a daily list. Write a letter to the universe. Create a screen play of your life. The next one is the law of command which states that with our words "We have the power to both destroy and heal words true and kind, they can change our world." Buddha.

Now, the law of command states that our words have the power to both destroy and heal. Words true and kind, they can change our world. We want to look at pronouncing everything in our life as good but understand that the law of command brings about manifestation in your world through your words, affirmations, declarations, and incantations that you command through your words.

You affirm through your words. You declare it just like the founding fathers declared the Declaration of Independence. You can declare your declaration a financial independence and it can be effective in your mind, your body, and your affairs. It is also known as autosuggestion, which is a way of using the law of command by repeating things over and over again. They start to go into your subconscious mind and as a result when they go into your subconscious mind, the subconscious is connected into your superconscious, which is where all manifestations come from. The Creative

Intelligence, the Universal Source that creates worlds, and all of the abundance that we see around us.

The same Creative Intelligence you have inside of you. It's just a matter of being happy, in tuning in, and turning on and getting out of the way, and allowing the universe to manifest in your daily life. They say that they're three steps for manifestation: 1) Ask, 2) Receive, and 3) Allow. Most of us know how to ask, very few of us know how to receive, and allowing is a big thing because of our discordant thoughts and limiting beliefs. I own my negative thoughts and the limiting beliefs keeps my mind in the forest monkey mind all over the place as opposed to taking it into a laser beam so that the universe can provide it's literally just like going to a restaurant.

You don't just say give me food, you say give me the salad the baked potato whatever it is that you want and you put in an order and you wait. You have expectancy. You have to say that it will come and what happens because of the training and the conditioning and the stresses we feel that we have to do everything. In fact, the truth is all we have to do is ask and receive, and basically get out of our own way. Not ask and make it happen, ask and work hard, but because of those conditionings that is what we do.

So one of the greatest well Secrets of the Soul concerning finances is to ask. You have already received, and then get out of your own way, which is your ego's way. And be open and receptive, thankful, appreciative, and gracious. And just giving gratitude and allowing the universe giving you goods and God are synonymous and that little birthright is prosperity and abundance. We are born rich but there's a whole process. A step again to that state of consciousness stepping into that good. The words have prospering power. So be very selective in what you say.

The next one is the law of command. The law of increase will always turn the tide. You are always using increase or decrease in your life and affairs; might as well use the increase. And you want to maintain an attitude of rich increase towards everything and everybody; everything and everybody prospers me now and I Prosper everything and everybody now.

Thinking of yourself or others, let the thought of riches, prosperity, success, goodness, and greatness breeze in magnificence. And your victorious good be the main thoughts within your mind because like attracts like, and the only thing that you really have control over is your own mind. Everything in relative existence is always changing, but you can have mastery over your own mind, if you can hold the thought, hold the vision long enough. Not that long, some prosper teachers say 64 seconds. That by law has to manifest because we're all connected and everything comes from a thought, from an idea.

Everything is made up of atoms and molecules. Everything is part of the quantum field, the unified field. So one effect in one part of the field will affect the other part of the cell and remember everything is within us and around us. Going back to that ancient saying, "As above, so below. As within, so without." Therefore, life flows from us and not to us. What is an "Awakened Life?" To "Be" totally happy, to wake up every day feeling fulfilled, grateful, thankful, and full of love, light, and bliss; to be awake, aware, and vibrantly alive.

So let's get into what being awakened really is. Sometimes it's referred to as enlightenment, God realization, self-actualization, to be one with the universe, and Nirvana. We're not talking about the way out mystical sense, we're talking about a practical everyday reality to be totally in harmony with your mind/body. To have a holistic state of consciousness and having your brain lit up (Brain Illumination) and coherence throughout your whole system.

So, the main points we're going to be looking at is: 1) being enlightened, 2) heaven on Earth, 3) what's possible, 4) the field of all possibilities, 5) being totally in tune with yourself in your environment, 6) being "Happy for No Reason," 7) a sense of fulfillment 24/7, 8) being excellent and naturally in Peak Performance, 8) looking good, feeling good, and smelling good in all areas of your life, 9) having your senses supercharged and the perfect and harmonious functioning between your mind and your body. Okay so let's jump in.

Now, in my own life I was blessed with a stupendous life changing experience. When I went to Ethiopia, West Africa, at the base of the Blue Nile for teacher training in the Transcendental Meditation Technique, a deep dive for three months curbing back into myself again and again. The whole process of meditation and activity, like dying a cloth, put into the sun to fade, and then put back into the sun again until its color fast.

Going deeper and deeper within my own experience so that I could help and relate to others as they grow and expand from the inside out. Also by going deep within my own consciousness, I started to experience higher and higher states of consciousness. As a result I was starting to have a major awakening based on experience, not intellectual understanding. Even though we were taught the intellectual understanding, we were also having profound inner experiences.

For knowledge to be complete, one must have an intellectual understanding as well as personal experience. We were undergoing a process termed "rounding" or alternations of meditation and activity many times a day in the morning and evening. The process starts early in the morning when it's still dark outside about 5:00 o'clock – 6:00 o'clock in the morning. We would do some exercises called asanas to stretch the body, called yoga asanas and then a very short breathing exercise called pranayama. Then we would meditate.

We would do a series of these in the morning, have lunch and then do a series of those in the afternoon have dinner and then evening a meeting of knowledge. This whole experience dissolves the stress in the nervous system and expands our consciousness. We literally went up in rounds as much as 12 rounds in the morning and 12 rounds in the afternoon early evening going from 1x1 to 2x2 to three on three, etc., all the way up to 12 on 12. This process is so amazing that I had one of the greatest experiences of my life. I literally was meditating one day and my whole consciousness just opened up into unbounded awareness, infinite, eternal.

I could see, feel, and know everything in 360°. In fact, this experience was so awesome that my consciousness expanded to encompass the entire universe and beyond. I was the sun, the moon, the stars, the galaxies, the cluster of the galaxies, the whole universe, and the universes within the Universes known as the Omniverse. I was all that ever was or all that ever will be. I was that and more. Yet the experience was just natural.

I literally was everything and the nothing from my perspective. I was the omnipresent, omnipotent of God. I was experiencing God consciousness. In fact, I was God consciousness and I could see, feel, think, and know everything simultaneously and I was everything and everything that was to be all in the here and now. I was experiencing everything simultaneously and everything just felt all right and full of love, unconditional love, light, and bliss. It lasted for about an hour and it was so real that when I came out of my meditation and I looked at my human body and saw this bag of skin and bones I couldn't believe it that I was reduced to just being in this little form of a human being because I was everything. Now I had the perception that I was reduced to just being a human being, but I had the experience of being everything of being the entire universe. So by having that experience, it changed my whole perception of life and I know who I am now. It so enlivened the passion in me to help others to know who they are. To know the truth and the truth will set you free based on experience, not mood making, not hallucination, not dreaming but actually experience higher states of consciousness.

We all have that capability within us - the kingdom of heaven is within. Upon returning from Ethiopia and having that experience of internalizing my whole being, that experience that all of life is an inside job, that experience of be still and know that I am God, the experience of having higher states of consciousness. Instead of having a headache and having to take a Tylenol know that I am the light of lights, pure consciousness for all of mankind. On a level of knowing this from experience, it has completely changed my life.

In fact, the shamans, masters, gurus, great beings from time immemorial have referred to this state as enlightenment that your brain is lit up. And that's how I felt. I was just so awake, so full, so naturally in the state of being, in the state of isness - the state of enlightenment. This state of enlightenment not being some mystical way out of a hallucinogenic dream but literally the perfect and harmonious functioning of the mind and the body. That brings about a holistic state of consciousness, where your brain is lit up of all of your energy centers online. You're completely coherent. The front and the back and the right and left hemispheres of the brain are in total coherence and you're literally experiencing heaven on Earth from the inside out.

Remember that the translation was Heavens with an "s" on it, which is a Greek translation for the expansion of the mind. In fact, one of the great quotes from a highly regarded teacher is that "the mouth of God is the mind of man." So at that level, your mind is totally expanded so you can tap in, tune in, and turn on your greatness. The stress is removed from the body and literally the nervous system is wired, fired, and inspired.

Everything in life is based on perception; your perception in your living temple, your body, it's determining how balanced and how stress-free your nervous system is. And the human system sometimes referred to as the "Tree of Life" inverted through your spine and your nervous system is like a mirror with dust on it. So if you get in front of the mirror, unless you take the dust off you will not get a clear reflection. So, that's the experience in life from the wear and tear in the fast-paced society. The conditionings up to when you're seven-years old and all of life's experiences leaves these imprints, these stresses on your system.

The process in Ethiopia was getting the dust off so that I could have a clear reflection and that was my experience. Another analogy is even though there are clouds in the sky, the sun can pierce through especially if you have many openings. So that was experienced in Ethiopia, where we were creating those openings, we were getting stress off of the system by deep meditation and then some activity and then some more.

Just going deeper and deeper within our own selves and as a result the mind gets expanded, the stress is removed from the body the body becomes much more resilient. The nervous system and you find that you don't incur stress as easily as you did before. So, what happens is you go from a state of limitation to a state of possibilities. A state of expansion. A state of the unified field. As a result your life changes. Where the world isn't just wear and tear and you not just going from birthday to birthday and just paying bills and getting old and dying. You start to transcend.

I mean you literally get out of the Matrix. You get out of the collective unconsciousness and you transcend. You go beyond and we all have that capability if you're a human being on this planet. With the nervous system you have the ability to literally walk on sunbeams and moonbeams and fly throughout the universe at will in your human body. Now I know that sounds outrageous and crazy, but we are that powerful, but you have to realize it, do the work of purifying your nervous system, expanding your mind and step into your greatness. Step into that field of all possibilities and get out of the field of death to get out of the field of the constant change because of the nature of everything in relative 3D existence is change.

You can either buy into that change or you can transcend it. You can get out of it, you can go above and beyond, you can escalate, you can elevate, and you can reach higher states of consciousness. We have free will where self-directed humans are the only beings that have the ability to change their course of life. In the wintertime the Canadian geese fly south. It can't say well I'm not going to the South this year, I'm going over to Europe. It functions from instinct. Humans are self-aware, they can make any choice, in·this free will universe. So you can choose to stay where you are, or you can choose to go higher. A fully realized Being once said, "Humans can go to some of the highest heights, to an average level, or go down to the animal level or below."

It's your choice, but the way we've set it up in this universe or if you want to say the way that God our source set it up is that there's karma. You reap what you sow. What goes around, comes around. For every action there is an equal and opposite reaction. As we talked about earlier, if you choose to go below, then you are going to attract pain, suffering, lack, and limitation.

If you choose to go higher, you can go to the level of a fully realized human being. You could be self-actualized. You could be one with the universe and then it's a whole different experience because the world is as you are. And from that level, you're tapped in, tuned in, and turned on. You're balanced with your environment. You're living 100% of the inner and 1% of the outer instead of just 5% - 10% of your mental conscious awareness. You find that you're fulfilled regardless of any outer circumstances because you're establishing yourself.

You're not locked into the ego, which is sometimes referred to as Edging God Out, so you find that your fulfillment is great. You go to those levels of happiness inside of yourself naturally and always feel happiness within. And the only thing that keeps you from being there all the time is the stress. So when you dissolve the stress, you start to have the experience of fullness is all that I am. And you find yourself in the state of happiness, of joy, of bliss and of all the noble things and characteristics that have been said over the centuries, over the eons about those Noble thoughts. God and good have been synonymous for eons. So you start establishing that goodness, that greatness, that magnificence, and then you start to find yourself being happy for no reason living a life of contribution, service, philanthropy, and as your cup runneth over you're sharing that and then you're living; do unto others as you would have them do unto you.

You start treating your brother and sister as you would have yourself treated at the highest and the best level because you have all your tools. As we related to earlier, you can't play a piano if you only have one tenth of your fingers; you can only make a little tune. You can never master the piano, could never create a concert, or a symphony, but you can take all ten of your fingers and master the game of life to be a victor instead of a victim.

In fact, one of the acronyms for love which is the only definition in the great sacred book is that God is love, and "love" being the light of victory everywhere. Love the light of victory everywhere so you become a victor instead of a victim because you're in tune with all the laws of nature. So the laws of nature support you as opposed to you violating the laws unconsciously and then certain imbalances come back.

The universe is irrespective of age, gender, color, and their loss. We talked about some of those laws and they're just as pliable as gravity and magnetism. You start using the laws and you start stepping up to your greatness, to your magnificence, and you start to be fulfilled and living an awakened life. As the great Reverend Ike said, "Look good, feel good, and smell good."

So most people think that I am physiologically younger than my chronological age. In fact, most places I go people are surprised by my chronological age. Most people call me a young man or they think I'm one of the youngest because I have worked on myself. I have reversed the aging process and I'm literally living an ageless life. I don't age. I use that as a choice that I make and I have the power to make that and so do you. There's nothing inevitable in the universe. In fact, most people think that death and taxes are inevitable, but that's only a little venire aspect of the mistake of the intellect. And, yes, if you're only using 5% - 10% of your mental potential and you are stressed out; yes, you basically just get old and die. You have disease and something will take you out of here, but if you take the high road and remembrances of the Free Will Universe, then it's the field of all possibilities.

So you can be at ease, as opposed to dis-ease and you can ascend, as opposed to having something to take you out. Actually there's a tribe, way up in the Himalayas, called the Hunzas. The average age of a man is about 110-120 years old. The average woman dies out between 60 or 70 while the men still sired children in their hundreds and run up and down the mountains. So why is this disparity between men and women? Most men end up with two or three wives in their lifetime because the wives die out and in this culture the women do all the work, the women get stressed out.

Men basically eat fresh organic fruits and vegetables, drink alkaline spring water, do a little wrestling, walk up and down the mountains, and make love. So they live a long time. Some scientists have said that is because of their water and because of their natural diet. Some say it's because of the apricots in that area. In reality it's taking the stress off of the men and allowing them to be maintained in a high level of wellness.

It's just like if a person puts a Model T in a garage, and takes good care of it by tuning the engine, change the oil, give it top maintenance. Then that Model T is preserved, and is still around today. But, if you treat it like most cars, and just drive and drive, just wear and tear, never really put it in the garage, then it's going to break down. The human system is the same way. So take the time to de-stress yourself. Take the time to transcend. Go to deeper levels within yourself. Take the time to go within, and as a result you will be awake, aware, and vibrantly alive.

8

An Awakened Life

In an awakened life you are totally in tune with your environment, living 200% of life: 100% of the inner and 100% of the outer. Be in fullness, regardless of the outer circumstances, and have the experience of fulfillment. Be totally full, happy, and content. Never go into disappointment, having the experience of "fullness is all that I am." Wake up every day, giving thanks for another great day, where everything is going my way. Literally become awake, aware, and vibrantly alive.

We've just had a walk down the yellow brick road. Wat have we seen and experienced as we've gone to the valleys and the mountaintops? Well, first of all we started with chapter one-

Life is an Inside Job - and it really is. If you don't get anything else out of this book, really take that to heart, and start to live from the inside out. Then we went into the mind, the Secrets of the Mind, and how powerful the mind is and the various levels of the mind from the conscious to the subconscious to the super conscious. The mind is much more powerful than the body, yet we need the balance between the two. Then we went further into the reality that we really have five bodies: 1) a mental body, 2) a physical body, 3) an emotional body (dealing with relationships) including ourselves; the greatest, which is with ourselves and then we have 4) a spiritual body, and 5) a financial body.

So we went from the secrets of the mind to the secrets of the body and then because we have to interact in life and interact with ourselves, we started on the emotions the energy in motion. The greatest relationship that you have is with yourself and from that relationship you deal with everything and everybody else, which was Chapter 5. Throughout this book we were looking at all of the various portals, which were five portals. A portal as you know is something that you go through, something that you have an opportunity to expand through. Just like in the Fairy tale Ali Baba and the 40 Thieves, when "Open Sesame" was said, the mountain would open up..

So then we went into the spiritual secrets. One of the most spiritual things being your thoughts and all the unseen experiences that we have in our lives. So, we went into secrets of financial freedom, briefly covered the six prosperity laws and the four laws of wealth that was Portal 5, chapter 7 and then we went into chapter 8. An awakened life, what all of this is leading up to for an overall Wealth Secrets of the Soul and through the acronym SOUL taking to heart these wonderful insights and innerstandings and then applied action. It could bring about success, opulence, unity, abundance, and love.

So, a few of the takeaways from each chapter are: Chapter 1, Life is an Inside Job. Every human being has infinite potential within them - you are the greatest! And the highest and best thing you can do is raise your vibration every day in every way. Chapter 2, Open Sesame, open up your awareness, and open up your heart to the beauty, magnificent, and glory within you. And we looked at the five portals which are: mental, emotional, physical, spiritual, and financial. We looked at how we could blossom, elevate, escalade, and ascend in all of those areas.

Then starting in Chapter 3 we went into the portals. The first one being Secrets of the Mind. We looked at the mental potential of most people on the planet being 5% - 10% and how one of the main secrets is using the other 90% - 95%. We looked at one of the simplest and easy ways to tap into that additional potential is through meditation. I recommend a technique that I teach called Transcendental Meditation, because it's so simple, so easy, and you get a deeper state of rest than you get doing 8 hours of sleep. The mind is awake, aware, and expanding, which brings about a state of restful alertness. As a result it's easy for you to tap into that other 90% to 95% naturally, and dissolve the stress in the human nervous system that's inhibiting the full potential of everyone.

Then we looked at Chapter 4, Portal 2, and Secrets of the Body. We looked at peak performance, mind/body coordination, youthing vs aging, and bliss attacks vs. heart attacks. Next, we looked at Secrets of Relationships, which was Portal 3. And we looked at the greatest relationship, which is within ourselves. Where we refer to self-referral, self-love, and then from that level experience positive uplifting relationships with everyone and everything else. Next we looked at Chapter 6 for the Spiritual Secrets. We tapped into our Creative Intelligence by transcending, and going beyond limiting beliefs, thus enabling us to manifest things better in our lives.

We finished with an Awakened Life. Living truly well, living fully in the light of your own brain illumination - Enlightenment, instead of just existing and reacting. We spontaneously take it as "come, take it easy," as opposed to living stressed. We naturally find ourselves responding to all of our experiences in a superfluid way.

"Life is a bowl of Cherries, just stay out of the pits."

Now that we have highlighted each chapter, let's look at some takeaways based on experiences from myself, clients, and colleagues over the years. Some good takeaways from the opening chapter to really remember: you're not your mind, you're not your body. You're not your intellect, and you're not your ego.

You are the witness or observer behind all these great tools. Your body is your living temple, but you're not your body. You are the soul, the spirit, the consciousness that inhabits your body that uses your mind, your intellect, your ego. You do this all from within, the "Kingdom of Heaven" is within - within your mind, within your heart, within your body, within all aspects of your Self. Again one of the reasons why we recommend meditation so much is that you start to have that experience just by being still.

Remember the third law of thermodynamics that states when the system goes down to absolute zero, the entropy goes out. Entropy is disorder, entropy is dis-ease. Entropy is stress. Removing the stress is like taking the weeds out of the garden. So, as long as you give yourself sunshine, water, fertilizer (experiences in life) and focus on what you want and not what you don't want, then life can be a very wondrous thing. A few takeaways from Chapter 2 is always be a student. Open up your mind and heart to learn to grow and to expand. Remember the more you love, the more you evolve, the more you evolve, the more you love. L-O-V-E spelled backwards is E-V-O-L.

Just a little acronym to help you to remember the beauty of living a life full of LOVE. You're both growing and evolving, or you are stagnating and dying. Even though you have over 350 trillion cells in your body, 98% to 99% of them die, and are replaced every year. Yet your spiritual blueprint keeps you together, so to speak. Even though we see ourselves and feel ourselves as being solid, technically we're not. In fact, if you look under a microscope at your body, your skin, and your bones, all your organs that you think are solid when you look under the microscope, they're anything but. It's just atoms and molecules rotating around space, not solid at all.

So one of the greatest Wealth Secrets of the Soul, which we discussed, was that you're not a human being that once in a while has a spiritual experience, but you are a spiritual being having a human experience.

You are a Spiritual Being having a Human Experience.

Now, it's up to you to realize this. Go in and change the programming that was passed on to you by your family, society, teachers, friends, everyone and everything that had an impact on you. That's what this book is about giving you some insight, some tools, some techniques so that you can be awake, aware, and vibrantly alive. Then as we moved on, we looked at some of the financial freedom secrets. We looked at the various universal laws and the applications. The points to remember are that the same UNIVERSAL MIND (Creative Intelligence) that created this universe is also within you.

You are a creator of your own reality and that you are co-creating all the time whether you're conscious or unconscious of it. The same thing applies to money, wealth, and riches. So whether you're rich or poor or in between it has to do with your consciousness. Whether you are in a prosperous state of consciousness, prosperity consciousness, or in scarcity consciousness. It's up to you. It has nothing to do with the outer circumstances. Even though just about everyone gets caught up in appearances because that is the way that we have been trained, conditioned.

That's just like if your car will not turn right. You get out of the car trying to move a big thousand-pound car from the outside when you can just with one finger from the inside turn it with power steering. The power steering is inside all of us. It's just a matter of reprogramming your Self, dissolving the stress, eliminating the dis-stress, and expanding our minds. This we can do pretty easily just by sitting in a chair 20 minutes, twice a day. But we have to do something otherwise the system remains the same and then it starts to break down, otherwise known as aging and dis-ease.

Finally, we can live an awakened life; a life full of joy, a life full of bliss, harmony, along with appreciation, gratitude, and thanks. Being happy every day in every way regardless of our circumstances - this is living in an awakened life, which we all have the potential to do. So I invite you to step forward and be the best that you can be. Make some swings. You'd be surprised by the home runs that you would hit and how life gets better and better until your "good is better and your better is best."

In Conclusion

DESIGN YOUR LIFE

I would like to encourage you to step forward. To stand up to be bold. Take hold of your own life and design your life. Design your life to be the best that you can be to be noble, to be great, to be magnificent, to use your magnificent mind to inspire, uplift, and awaken yourself, know thyself, and then let your cup runneth over to help all around you.

Your family, friends, city, nation, and world.

Remember, "The World is As You Are."

As you become fuller, more conscious, more loving, more kind, and more generous you naturally start changing the world. As a matter of fact, the only way that we can have world peace is that each individual is peaceful and fulfilled within their own lives, because the forest is only as green as each individual tree. When you look at a green forest, it's because every tree is green. So as we realize our full potential and maximize our evolution, it's reflected in our world. So, one of the greatest things that you can contribute to world peace is to have peace within your own "Self." Now, as you know the human experience abounds with high mountain tops to low valley experiences. A nice way to categorize this is that life is full of challenges. So, just like I overcame many things, all of us are overcoming magnanimous challenges, and everyday challenges. Sometimes it's hard to just get out of bed, but we can find that strength within ourselves to overcome and uplift anything. As I mentioned before, "Life is an Inside Job."

So, all the creativity, all of the intelligence, all of the energy that we could ever expect is waiting for us to unlock the key to our greatness, to a fully lived life and it wants to encourage you. Just like the pioneers of the early part of this country pushed forward through all types of obstacles. You can also be a pioneer within your own consciousness to make it to the promised land of life, liberty, and the pursuit of happiness.

I've been in your shoes with everyday challenges and I still have some. But the beauty is every day in every way I'm getting better and better, and it feels so good. Regardless of what happens in your life, make it a priority to feel good, happiness for no reason. It's a state that you literally have control over. You can't control your circumstances, but you can control your own mind, your own inner landscape. It takes some work because the ego gets involved, emotions flare, and conscious thinking, which is a storehouse of memories, can easily cause some unfulfillment. Yet we can overcome, we can ascend, and hopefully this book is giving you some insight into your greatest fears.

Remember the quote we emphasized earlier in this book from Nelson Mandela? "Our greatest fear is not our inadequacies. Our greatest fear is that we are powerful beyond measure." Being more direct, we've all heard the saying 'to err is human." The statement is off when you realize your full potential because the truth of the matter is to be human is to be perfect; to be human is to be divine. All of us have a spark of divinity within us, the spark of the Creator, the spark of the universe, and literally all we have to do is come into contact with it. Tap in, tune in, and turn on to realize your full potential. It's just like watering a plant.

"You water the root to enjoy the fruit."

Water is the inside job when you start to blossom from the inside out. I have been teaching meditation for decades and I've been to 35 countries. I've been to just about every major city in the US and I've seen it time and time again blossoming from the inside out. I have taught the richest of the rich, the poorest of the poor, doctors, lawyers, teachers, merchants, and chiefs. It doesn't matter your gender, doesn't matter your background, doesn't matter if you're illiterate or smart, as long as you are human and have a nervous system, the third law of thermodynamics works for you. When the system goes to absolute zero, the entropy goes out of the system, the distress, the disorder, the disease goes out.

And what's left is the brilliant, magnificent, marvelous, stupendous you. You deserve to be all that you can be. So, I encourage you to take little steps forward every day and you will start to see the dust coming off the mirror. You'll start to see the clear reflection. And as a result, you'll find yourself being more thankful or grateful and you'll have so much love, creativity, intelligence, and energy that it starts to pour over to your fellow man. You barely had time to take care of yourself and your own family in the past, but now you start to find that you can contribute. You can give back to society, above and beyond your own immediate family, because you just have so much to give. You tapped into that reservoir that overflows.

I'd like to invite you to our website:

www.RealWealthInstitute.org

Here you find a digital version of all Urban Knowledge Centers. We will assist you mentally, emotionally, physically, spiritually, and financially, and we have experts from around the world to coach you, guide you, and enlighten you.

Join our family of rising avatars - fully realized human beings. We have a membership site covering all five portals. We call it the "WHOW" portal that has all five portals: Wealth, Health, Opulence, and Wisdom in our Real Wealth Urban Knowledge Centers. When we reach a thousand members or more in our online portal, in every major city, we'll build a green sacred geometry, naturally off the grid building. Where you can meditate, study, (there will be quiet/meditation rooms, and the Hall of Knowledge for live lectures and group meditations, which is also a part of your membership.) So you'll have techniques available to you online from the comfort of your home or you can physically go to a 'Know thy Self" Urban Knowledge Center.

Series
of Knowledge Books

W e are also coming forth with the "Secret of the Soul" Series: Health Secrets of Soul, Love Secrets of the Soul, Success Secrets of the Soul, and Wisdom Secrets of the Soul. You can contact me. Thank you so much for taking the time to read my book. Hopefully, you gained at least one thing from this book that can make a difference in your life. Our goal is to impact the lives of countless people around the globe starting right here, at home, in the urban cities of America.

To be a lighthouse in the dark areas of our society, and then stretch out to every human being that is experiencing stress and strain in their nervous system in America, and around the world. I wish you the highest and best in mind, body, and affairs in life. In general, I know that you will step into your greatness. Just like Muhammad Ali used to say, "You are the greatest!"

Thank you and farewell for now!

Made in the USA
Middletown, DE
21 January 2021